helping new people find their place in your church

welcome & enfold

JEFF STAM

Leader Guide

CRC Publications
Grand Rapids, Michigan

Unless otherwise indicated, the Scripture quotations in this publication are from the HOLY BIBLE, NEW INTERNATIONAL VERSION, © 1973, 1978, 1984, International Bible Society. Used by permission of Zondervan Bible Publishers.

Welcome & Enfold: Helping New People Find Their Place in Your Church, © 1999 by CRC Publications, 2850 Kalamazoo Ave. SE, Grand Rapids, MI 49560. All rights reserved. With the exception of brief excerpts for review purposes, no part of this book may be reproduced in any manner whatsoever without written permission from the publisher. Printed in the United States of America on recycled paper. ✪ We welcome your comments. Call 1-800-333-8300 or e-mail us at editors@crcpublications.org.

ISBN 1-56212-494-3

10 9 8 7 6 5 4 3 2 1

Contents

Introduction 5

Groundwork 9

1 Going Out—Bringing In 11

2 How Are We Doing? 15

3 "Welcome to _____ Church. We're Truly Glad You're Here." 19

4 Moving from Reaching to Enfolding New Members 25

Continuing Task Force 31

Appendix A   Questionnaires and Survey Tools 33

Appendix B   Resources 45

Introduction

A Biblical Model

In the Great Commission (Matt. 28:19), Jesus mandates the original eleven members of the New Testament church to go out in order to make disciples of people from all backgrounds. These people were not merely to remain new converts to Christianity. They were to be claimed and sealed with baptism in the name of the triune God. They were to belong to God. They were to be God's disciples. The implications of this commitment were many. It meant change—a new identity and a new family, and, as the simple chorus states, *no turning back.* Salvation is eternal. It is also all-encompassing. It is meant to be experienced in the context of Christ's body, the church.

We get a picture of new disciples being enfolded into the fledgling church early in its history:

> Those who accepted [Peter's] message were baptized, and about three thousand were added to their number that day. They devoted themselves to the apostles' teaching and to the fellowship, to the breaking of bread and to prayer. Everyone was filled with awe, and many wonders and miraculous signs were done by the apostles. All the believers were together and had everything in common. Selling their possessions and goods, they gave to anyone as he had need. Every day they continued to meet together in the temple courts. They broke bread in their homes and ate together with glad and sincere hearts, praising God and enjoying the favor of all the people. And the Lord added to their number daily those who were being saved (Acts 2:41-47).

This was family. They were committed to each other and to their common cause and calling. They wanted to be together, to worship and learn and feast and fellowship. Outsiders saw this and wanted in. The apostle Paul talks about this marvelous bringing together of people (even Gentiles) as a great mystery (Eph. 3:6). In 1 Corinthians 12, Paul uses the analogy of the body to describe the church:

> The body is a unit, though it is made up of many parts; and though all its parts are many, they form one body. So it is with Christ. For we were all baptized by one Spirit into one body—whether Jews or Greeks, slave or free—and we were all given the one Spirit to drink.
>
> Now the body is not made up of one part but of many. If the foot should say, "Because I am not a hand, I do not belong to the body," it would not for that reason cease to be part of the body. And if the ear should say, "Because I am not an eye, I do not belong to the body," it would not for that reason cease to be part of the body. If the whole body were an eye, where would the sense of hearing be? If the whole body were an ear, where would the sense of smell be? But in fact God has arranged the parts in the body, every one of them, just as he wanted them to be. If they were all one part, where would the body be? As it is, there are many parts, but one body.
>
> The eye cannot say to the hand, "I don't need you!" And the head cannot say to the feet, "I don't need you!" On the contrary, those parts of the body that

seem to be weaker are indispensable, and the parts that we think are less honorable we treat with special honor. And the parts that are unpresentable are treated with special modesty, while our presentable parts need no special treatment. But God has combined the members of the body and has given greater honor to the parts that lacked it, so that there should be no division in the body, but that its parts should have equal concern for each other. If one part suffers, every part suffers with it; if one part is honored, every part rejoices with it.

Now you are the body of Christ, and each one of you is a part of it (1 Cor. 12:12-27).

The body of Christ is meant to be together, individual members in their special, God-determined places doing their God-determined tasks that make the body whole and healthy. This is the goal of the welcoming and enfolding process.

Present Reality Confronting the Church

When members of the body do not fully participate, the body cannot fully function. It will limp along and continually bump into things. It will not be able to see and hear well enough to fully represent Christ to the world.

Welcoming and enfolding people into the church, the topic of this study, is not just about reaching the lost. Nor is it solely about church growth or closing the "back door" in an attempt to cut attrition rates. It is about the church being everything Christ intended it to be, both to itself and to the world around it. Christ was concerned that the church live in unity and oneness (John 17:21) and that it model love so that people would identify church members as disciples of Jesus (John 13:35).

Unfortunately the model of the early church in Acts, Paul's description of a fit, fully functioning body, and Christ's desire that the church be characterized by unity and love are not true of many churches today. The title of the book *Finding Them, Keeping Them* by Gary McIntosh and Glen Martin says it well. While we may have found a very effective evangelism tool or have exciting programs and side-door ministries that bring many people into the church, assimilation as participants in the church family does not happen automatically. It requires desire, planning, action, and constant evaluation. The purpose of this study is to help you and your church be proactive and purposeful about welcoming and enfolding.

This study is a revision of *How to Warmly Welcome and Effectively Enfold People in Your Church*. In the years since that material was developed, enfolding frequent visitors and also members into active participation in the church has certainly become no easier. In the new millennium, the church will hardly have time to catch its breath as it tries to keep up with the rapid changes of North American society and the resulting needs of those to whom it ministers.

George Barna has stated that our North American culture completely transitions or "reinvents itself" every three to five years, while it takes the average church thirty to forty years to make a comparable transition. If Barna is correct, that likens the church to Sisyphus, a figure from Greek mythology who was condemned forever to roll a large boulder uphill. We never make real forward progress. Some churches are still trying to deal with social realities that emerged thirty or more years ago. One change that dramatically affects the ability of a church to enfold is the transience of society. The sociological impact of this change was being addressed in the mid-sixties. Many new visitors or members that come into your church today will not have the luxury of a long assimilation period. Churches may find that a growing number of their members have been around for only a few years.

Another major influence is busyness. The average individual's level of busyness will not likely diminish in the near future. Computer technology, which once promised more and more leisure time, has had quite the opposite effect. Because we are now able to do so much more, we do. And this is not only an adult phenomenon. Churches trying to incorporate and enfold children and teens find the competition for time and commitment to be formidable.

Long past for most churches are the days when welcoming and enfolding are easy because Johnny and Susie are a son and daughter of the church, or because Sue Ellen married into the church and became "one of us." Increasingly, people coming into the church will have less in common, even if they are next-door neighbors.

Churches must be purposeful about welcoming newcomers, no matter what door they use to enter the church. A warm welcome on the first visit may provide encouragement for visitors to return, but it will not be sufficient to make them continue to feel welcome. On their wedding day a husband and wife will speak of their love for each other, yet though the truth of those words may not change, each spouse needs to receive the expression of that love continually. It is not enough to assume that an individual feels welcomed because he or she came with a friend. The *whole church* must provide a genuine and ongoing welcome.

Enfolding, too, must be a conscious effort; it will not happen automatically over the course of time. The more people who are actively involved in welcoming and enfolding, the less chance that visitors or new members will fall victim to the assumption that "someone else must be responsible for them."

Working Toward Effective Solutions

Today, churches can be as different from one another as snowflakes or fingerprints, but there will always be several common bonds, such as doctrinal affinity, historical roots, and traditions. One common bond that we are assuming for this study is a desire and willingness to grow, to be salt and light, to make disciples, to be everything to every member (or guest) that Christ intends the church to be. You must not be willing to be "status quo." You must not allow demographics, transition, and outside pressures to force you into stagnation, deterioration, and death.

There are many facets involved in being a healthy, growing church. Effective welcoming and enfolding, by themselves, will not be sufficient. Without them, however, health and growth will be impossible.

Using *Welcome and Enfold*

Welcome and Enfold is designed to be used in a variety of settings. You may choose to present this material in an adult church school class, a small group discussion, or in a seminar or weekend retreat. Its versatility is one of this course's strengths. The success of *Welcome and Enfold* can be measured directly both to the final follow-through of the participants and to the groundwork focusing on your church's current welcoming and enfolding efforts. The guidelines and tools necessary for that task are laid out in the next section, Groundwork. The results of this advance work will provide the basis for the first session.

The preliminary work and the follow-up tasks are the responsibility of the Welcome and Enfold task force. In the Groundwork section, you will find the specific responsibilities of this task force. In addition to the task force, there will be a facilitator who will lead each of the four sessions. The facilitator should be a member of the task force, but does not need to be the leader of the task force. It is important that the facilitator *know the material well*. He or she should carefully go through *all* the material in advance. Each session builds on the previous one, but because of possible time constraints or a desire to focus more on certain issues the facilitator needs to know where adjustments can be made. There is no problem if one session flows into the next or a discussion has to be continued (if the facilitator considers it to be important enough) the next time. The facilitator does need to know what's coming up so as to be able to prioritize time. Although the content is presented in four sessions, the material can easily be expanded into more sessions to allow for more in-depth discussion.

Pedagogically, there are some advantages to using *Welcome and Enfold* in a seminar or retreat setting. That setting allows for more focus and small group dynamics. Also, discussion or brainstorming sessions can usually be given more time in a retreat setting. If done in a seminar or retreat, plan for about eight hours of teaching and discussion time. Whatever setting or format you choose, remember that this material is designed to be a tool, not a master. Feel free to adapt and mold in a way that best fits your needs and circumstances.

This study focuses on the following areas:
- biblical foundations for welcoming and enfolding
- understanding your community and church
- looking at your church's current efforts and effectiveness
- principles for effective welcoming and enfolding
- individual involvement in welcoming and enfolding
- corporate involvement in welcoming and enfolding

What Next?

By the end of the four sessions, the group should have come up with a number of measurable ideas that can increase your church's effectiveness in welcoming and enfolding. The task force will continue to work after the course is completed to develop an action plan that includes specific immediate and long-term goals. These goals should be clear, measurable, and specific enough to allow for evaluation every six to twelve months. Further training may be recommended, but there should be some steps, especially in the area of individual involvement, that can start immediately. The section "Continuing Task Force" on pages 31-32 offers some suggestions for a possible action plan.

The "My Part" form (p. 30) that is filled out by participants at the end of the final session invites those who are interested to continue on as part of this task force. So that the ideas don't get lost or forgotten, someone should take notes in each session, keeping a record of the discussion, particularly potential problem areas and new ideas. These notes will be valuable resources for the task force.

May God bless your church's efforts to welcome and enfold each person into the body of Christ!

Groundwork

This *Welcome and Enfold* study is not intended to serve as just another topic for a four-week segment of adult church school. It is designed to be a versatile tool that can be used repeatedly in a number of different small group settings. Its main function is not simply to impart information; it is intended to be a catalyst for change. For some churches the necessary changes may be radical; for others, the study may affirm practices that already are in place, resulting only in slight, midcourse corrections.

Although mentioned together in the Introduction, the four sessions and the follow-through are two distinct phases of *Welcome and Enfold*. Much information will be brought to light. Some participants will do nothing with the information they receive. Others, however, will be eager to apply the concepts and work toward becoming more effective in welcoming and enfolding new people. All this implies a commitment that extends far beyond the time invested in going through the four-session study.

The Welcome and Enfold Task Force

Much of the success of *Welcome and Enfold* rests with the commitment of the Welcome and Enfold task force. The Welcome and Enfold task force is responsible for the entire program (groundwork, teaching, and follow-through). The task force should consist of at least four members of the congregation who have a gift for making people feel genuinely welcome in your church. The task force should include the facilitator of the course, the pastor of your church, and two other members. It would be helpful if the elders or council of your church would approve the members of the task force and empower them to develop a strategy for action at the conclusion of the course that would be part of an ongoing ministry plan. Upon completion of the course, the task force can be enlarged by adding study participants or re-formed for the purpose of developing a specific action plan.

Several weeks prior to the first session, the task force should gather the necessary data for discussion in the first session. This requires advance research in order to identify what is currently being done and its effectiveness. Appendix A includes questionnaires for visitors, new members, and former members to be used for gathering the data. A one-page summary should be written for each of the questionnaires.

Along with advance preparation should be advance promotion. It is essential that the pastor show support for the *Welcome and Enfold* endeavor. The pastor can make announcements that promote the sessions, participate in some of the preliminary surveys, and perhaps deliver one or two preparatory messages on the subject.

Three Critical Questions to Ask

Along with questions about what your church is currently doing, the task force must also address some basic questions about your church, such as

- Who are we?
- Where are we?
- What does God want us to be?

Who Are We?

The question of who you are will focus somewhat on demographic concerns: age, marital status, ethnicity, income, education, occupation, and so on. You will want to take special note of statistics that reveal large blocks that give a certain identity to your church: 80 percent of the adults are under the age of fifty; most have a college education; the majority are farmers; there are many single parents; and so on. You should then ask if any of these factors have changed significantly in the last five to ten years. For example, are there many more single parents than there were just a few years ago? Do you have fewer young people now than you used to have?

Is your church growing? Is it declining? Is it in a maintenance mode? Has there been any recent (in the last ten years) internal trauma, such as a split, a rapid succession of pastors, or external threats that have robbed people of hope and motivation? Negative, underlying currents, though unspoken, can put the brakes on the introduction and assimilation of new members to the body.

Where Has God Placed Us?

Understanding where you are as a church addresses some of the same questions as above. The difference is that the first question applies to those within your church family; now you are asking those questions of people outside your doors in your immediate neighborhood. If you are a rural church, your neighborhood may be a whole community, while an urban or suburban church can often draw the circle of natural impact a little tighter. It is especially important for urban and suburban churches to determine if membership is from the immediate neighborhood. If not, you'll want to ask if there was a change that occurred somewhere along the line and what factors (probably sociological) may have influenced that change.

Is the family make-up of the community *inside* your doors considerably different than the community just *outside* your doors? This is an important question to address. It deals with the church's ability and willingness to welcome and enfold immediate neighbors. With few exceptions (such as the megachurch whose membership comes from far and wide) there is little reason for a church to remain in a community it does not plan to reach.

The information necessary to understand your neighborhood can be gathered in various ways. The best technique is observation. Get out there! Observe people. Spend a half hour with a cup of coffee in the nearest fast-food restaurant. Who do you see? These are your neighbors. Meet them. Talk to them. Listen to them. Find out who they are. When people realize that you are interested in them without any strings attached, they usually will open up. Another way to observe your community is by means of prayer walking. As you and others walk through the community individually or in pairs, do so in an attitude of prayer. By observing with "praying eyes" you can learn much. Vehicles in the driveway, toys on the lawn, music, dish antennas, and home appearance are all clues about economic level, children, teen drivers, interests, leisure activities, and needs.

By using a well thought-out, low-key questionnaire (see Appendix A), you can canvass a neighborhood without a large investment in time and resources. Sociological mistrust and busyness can make canvassing a near impossibility, but it will work in some situations. Census statistics relative to your community are usually available through local government offices or public library. It will take a little research, but the information is usually readily available.

Another excellent resource for gathering demographic data on any community in the United States is a service called Percept. This service can provide detailed information and projections on a defined geographical area, based on latest census figures. It allows you to specify the kind of information you want and select a specific target area by a defined radius, zipcode area, or area you define by bordering roads on a map. (Call Christian Reformed Home Missions at 1-800-266-2175, ext. 762 for more information and an order form. In Canada, you may obtain a demographic profile by calling Outreach Canada at 604-272-0732.)

What Is Our Purpose?

The answer to "What does God want us to be?" is an important part of welcoming and enfolding. While you may be able to welcome someone into a church where purpose or vision is ill-defined, you won't be able to do so as enthusiastically as you could if you were sure of God's purpose for your church. Rick Warren, pastor of Saddleback Church in California, a rapidly growing church with attendance surpassing 10,000, refers to being "purpose driven." Without a well-defined purpose it becomes almost impossible to effectively enfold, because the perceptive participant will want to know what it is he or she is being asked to embrace.

There are many church growth books on the market. Authors are anxious to share strategies or models that have worked in their situation. Unfortunately, some imply (or their readers infer) that their particular spin, if applied in just the right way, will guarantee results. What is required prior to strategy is vision and purpose (an answer to the question "What does God want us to be?"). The church also must ask questions such as "Where are we going? Where do we hope to be in two, five, or ten years?" If the church has no destination in view, it's likely that the church will go nowhere.

Obviously, the task force cannot be responsible for the development of the church's purpose or vision statement; however, this information is important for the success of the task of welcoming and enfolding. The questionnaires in Appendix A will help the task force gain this information. Remember, you should have the necessary information from these surveys and any other diagnostic data summarized and available before beginning the first session with your group.

SESSION 1

Going Out—Bringing In

Setting

The setting for your four sessions together is important and will depend on the size of your group. If the group is small (twelve or less), a relaxed setting is appropriate. If your church has a lounge area, this would work well as long as it allows for the option of using an overhead projector and/or a whiteboard or chalkboard. If you have a larger group, chairs arranged in a semicircle creates a more relaxed setting and allows for greater participation. The teaching is structured to encourage dialogue, so your role is that of a facilitator rather than a lecturer. You will probably be able to assume this role more comfortably if you are seated in the circle; however, if the group is large, this may not be possible. Participants will be asked to write in their manuals, but it is probably better not to use tables, as this tends to create too formal a setting and spreads out the participants too much.

Session Length

The sessions should take about one hour. If you have less or more time than that, adjustments will need to be made. Obviously, more time can be given to any of the exercises or discussion time.

Purpose

This first session has two purposes. The first purpose is to develop a biblical basis for going out and bringing others in. We will look briefly at Christ's commission to his fledgling church to go out and at the implications of making disciples, baptizing, and teaching. We will also look at some of the patterns of early church life in Acts 2. Without recognizing the biblical foundation for the primacy of kingdom growth and development, which is normally realized in the context of the local church, your congregation will have no adequate reason to give high priority to the ministry of welcoming and enfolding others into the body of Christ.

The second purpose for this session is to take a look at who you are as a church and at the community you serve. This part of the discussion will be based on the preliminary research completed by the task force. At minimum, this should include a summary statement describing your church and the immediate community. Your purpose at this point is not to criticize the church or make excuses for unhealthy trends; rather, it is to present a factual snapshot of the current reality, positive or negative.

Necessary Materials
- overhead projector with blank transparencies, whiteboard, or a flip chart (depending on the size of your group)
- markers
- a copy of the summaries of the congregational and community surveys (Appendix A) prepared by the task force for each class participant
- student manual for each participant

Opening Prayer

Begin each class time with prayer. This will remind group members that they are about God's business; God will lead where people submit to his will. The purpose of each session is included in the student manual. You may want to draw attention to that before opening each session with prayer. That way the opening prayer can focus specifically on the material to be covered. Feel free to ask different participants to take part in the prayer time.

Welcome

Briefly welcome the participants to the study and make sure that everyone is where they intended to be, especially if there are other groups meeting at the same time. If the participants do not all know each other, have them introduce themselves. You may want to consider the option of name tags if the group is large and many of them don't know each other. The welcome time is necessary only for this first session. If new people come to succeeding sessions, briefly welcome them or have them introduce themselves if the rest of the group does not know them. If you have not already distributed the student manuals, do so now. Make sure that all group members have a pen and a Bible.

What God Says

Matthew 28:16-19

^{16}The eleven disciples went to Galilee, to the mountain where Jesus had told them to go. ^{17}When they saw him, they worshiped him; but some doubted. ^{18}Then Jesus came to them and said, "All authority in heaven and on earth has been given to me. ^{19}Therefore go and make disciples of all nations, baptizing them in the name of the Father and of the Son and of the Holy Spirit, ^{20}and teaching them to obey everything I have commanded you. And surely I am with you always, to the very end of the age."

Acts 1:6-7

^{6}So when they met together, they asked him, "Lord, are you at this time going to restore the kingdom to Israel?" ^{7}He said to them: "It is not for you to know the times or dates the Father has set by his own authority. ^{8}But you will receive power when the Holy Spirit comes on you; and you will be my witnesses in Jerusalem, and in all Judea and Samaria, and to the ends of the earth."

Ask one or two people to read the Scripture passages. Encourage group members to respond to the following questions:

1. **What similarities do you see between these two commands of Christ?**
   The participants are the same (Christ and his disciples), although these are two distinct events (Matthew 28 takes place in Galilee and Acts 1 on Mount Olivet, outside of Jerusalem). More important, however, is the command to go and tell others (make disciples, teach, and witness). Some may note that both passages involve authority and power. In Matthew Christ declares that all authority belongs to him, which he is now passing along to them (a commissioning implies the imparting of authority necessary to fulfill the responsibility), and in Acts the disciples are clearly told that they will go forth in the power of the Holy Spirit.

2. **In Matthew 18:19-20, what specific tasks are the disciples given? What limitations are placed upon them?**
   The disciples are to go, make disciples, baptize, and teach. In the original language, "go" is not as much a command as an assumption. A more accurate reading might be "While you are going [an assumed activity], disciple . . . baptize . . . teach." There are no implied limitations. In Acts all limitations—geographic, cultural, ethnic—are purposefully removed. The disciples are instructed to go to "the ends of the earth"—literally.

3. **What suggests that a long-term commitment is required?**
   While a specific methodology is not stated, it is clear that the level of involvement—the discipling process and teaching "everything I have commanded you"—requires long-term commitment. Baptism was not only a sign and seal of joining together with the triune God, it was a sign of joining together with Christ's body, the church (Eph. 4:4-5). Fulfilling these commands of Christ implies a long-term, mutual commitment.

4. **Since these commands were given to Jesus' disciples, are they applicable only to them? Why or why not?**
   No. Just as the later epistles to the churches apply to the church today, so too Jesus' words to his disciples are relevant and binding for us. If we suggest that some of Jesus' teachings do not apply to us, we place ourselves on very dangerous ground. We would then have to question the validity of the promises Jesus made to the disciples, which we readily accept for ourselves.

Acts 2:42-47

^{42}They devoted themselves to the apostles' teaching and to the fellowship, to the breaking of bread and to prayer. ^{43}Everyone was filled with awe, and many wonders and miraculous signs were done by the apostles. ^{44}All the believers were together and had everything in common. ^{45}Selling their possessions and goods, they gave to anyone as he had need. ^{46}Every day they continued to meet together in the temple courts. They broke bread in their homes and ate together with glad and sincere hearts, ^{47}praising God and enjoying the favor of all the people. And the Lord added to their number daily those who were being saved.

5. **What one word might you use to summarize this Scripture passage?**
   If you have an overhead or whiteboard, you may want to list some of the suggestions offered by the group mem-

bers. Possibilities include togetherness, communion, community, church, sharing, cooperation, body-life, and so on. After you have listed several, look for a common theme. You are trying to bring out the idea of oneness and unity.

6. **What evidence do you see that the early church was actively welcoming and enfolding new believers?**
List these in two columns with the headings "Welcoming" and "Enfolding" on the overhead or whiteboard. Group members may have more difficulty coming up with welcoming activities, but welcome was obviously a part of the early church because they were growing steadily on a daily basis.

A Look at Our Community and Ourselves
Small Group Interaction

For this part of the session, have the group break up into three smaller groups. Each group should have six to eight participants, but smaller or larger groups would work too. If your main group is very large, more than one small group could work on the same assignment. Have available the summaries of the preliminary groundwork done by the task force, but do not give the information to the small groups now. You are looking for their perceptions of reality. Don't let the groups move out too far from your meeting room because it becomes too difficult to gather everyone back together. Each group should assign someone to make a brief (two- to three-minute) report back to the larger group. You will want to limit small group time to eight to ten minutes. Group assignments are as follows:

Group 1—Describing Our Community

The task of this group is to write a description of what they perceive to be the church's target community. There may be immediate confusion as to what the church's target community is, but let them struggle with it. If your church would consider itself to be a neighborhood church, have them describe the church's immediate neighborhood. They won't have much time, so don't expect an in-depth paragraph. Have them write down key words, prioritizing them from most descriptive to least. Avoid giving too many hints. Part of the purpose of this exercise is to determine how the members naturally perceive the target community.

Group 2—Describing Our Church

The task of this group is to write a description of the church. This should not be a description of the "hoped-for" church or the church's goals and vision but of perceived reality. Like the first group, this group can choose to write a descriptive paragraph or a list of key words, prioritized from most to least descriptive. If they run stuck, a twist they could use would be to describe what their church is not (for instance, "Our church is not a megachurch that attracts a lot of visitors every week"). The purpose here is to be factual. Don't allow negative criticism of the church. There is no place for throwing mud at the bride of Christ. As with the first group, don't give too many hints; allow group participants to express their perspective.

Group 3—Church Growth Trends

The task of this group is to identify growth trends (increases or decreases) or changes in the church and community served. Have this group focus on changes or noticeable trends of the past five to ten years. Have them try to identify possible causes and a point in time when these changes began to occur. Again, avoid hints. You may need to give an example, but the work is theirs.

Reporting Back

Allow the representatives from all three groups to report back. Encourage the participants to take note of comments and key words on pages 11-12 in their books. In order to better control your time, allow all groups to report back before engaging in open discussion. As facilitator you may want to ask clarifying questions (for instance, what a specific term means), but don't ask for positions to be defended at this point.

You can hand out the congregational and community survey summaries prepared by the task force at this time. That information may confirm what the groups are reporting, but it is also possible that it will give a different picture. If you have time, allow for feedback and discussion of each group report before handing out the prepared material. This may help to avoid stifling active discussion, and you may find that the discussion serves as an excellent introduction to the summaries. If during the reporting sessions, however, you note that there are real differences, you will be better served by distributing the survey summaries immediately so the discussion time can be used to address the differences in perspective. You will have to judge how to handle the discussion based on the time available.

Community and Church Similarities and Differences

Using the overhead projector or whiteboard, draw two columns as shown below. After discussing the task force summaries, list in each column the agreed-upon descriptors or key words that reflect the current reality and trends for your community and church. Then use lines or colors to show the similarities and differences that exist between the two columns. Participants should record this information on page 12 in their books.

Community	Church

Assignment

For the next session, have the participants complete the questionnaire "Rating Our Welcoming and Enfolding Efforts" on pages 14-15 in their books. If you are not following a weekly schedule, be sure to remind the participants of the next meeting time.

Closing Prayer

Close this session with prayer in a way that is appropriate to your group and the time you have. You may want to focus your prayer on the discoveries made during the session, thanking God and asking for continued blessing on areas where your church is meeting needs in the community. You may want to request guidance if there are any major differences or a lack of identity with the community.

SESSION 2

How Are We Doing?

Purpose
The purpose for this session is to identify some key biblical passages on welcoming and enfolding. You will examine God's teaching regarding the drawing in of the nations, the practice of hospitality, and what it means to be the family of God and the body of Christ. You will also take a closer look at who you are as a church and how that becomes a factor in the way you welcome and enfold people into the body.

Using the task force's previously prepared summaries of visitor, new member, and former member questionnaires, you will attempt to measure the church's current verbal and non-verbal messages to newcomers and its effectiveness in drawing people into active participation. Based on these identified strengths and weaknesses, you will begin to develop some specific action plans for improvement.

Necessary Materials
- overhead projector with blank transparencies, whiteboard, or a flip chart
- markers
- list of key words and trends that identified the church from session 1—if possible, on an overhead transparency
- summaries of visitor, new member, and former member questionnaires (Appendix A)—if possible, on overhead transparencies

Opening Prayer
You or a member of the group should open with prayer. (If you ask a member of the group to pray, be sure to get that person's permission before you meet.) Focus on your purposes for this session.

What God Says
Genesis 12:1-3
¹The LORD had said to Abram, "Leave your country, your people and your father's household and go to the land I will show you.
²"I will make you into a great nation
    and I will bless you;
I will make your name great,
    and you will be a blessing.
³I will bless those who bless you,
    and whoever curses you I will curse;
and all peoples on earth
    will be blessed through you."

Psalm 67:3-4
³May the peoples praise you, O God; may all the peoples praise you. ⁴May the nations be glad and sing for joy, for you rule the peoples justly and guide the nations of the earth.

Ask willing group members to read the Scripture passages aloud (they are also printed in the student guides). Then ask the following questions. Guide the discussion by giving the group opportunity to express their views. You should not appear to have the only right answer.

1. **What does Genesis 12:3 tell us about God's purpose in choosing Abram and his descendants?**
   God elects Abram in order to make him a blessing for all the nations of the earth. God's chosen people enjoy many blessings. But their greatest blessing is that they may share God's goodness and God's saving love with all the nations of the earth. This foundational promise to Abram clearly reveals God's overarching desire and purpose to bless the whole world through mighty acts of redemption.

2. **This psalm is a prayer. What is being requested regarding the other peoples and nations? What does that imply?**
   The psalm writer prays that all peoples would praise God and all nations would sing for joy and be guided by God. This implies a relationship that is established between God and the other peoples and nations. It implies that they too belong to God and join together with Israel in bringing praise to God.

Matthew 25:35
"For I was hungry and you gave me something to eat, I was thirsty and you gave me something to drink, I was a stranger and you invited me in. . . ."

Romans 12:13
Share with God's people who are in need. Practice hospitality.

1 Peter 4:8-10
⁸Above all, love each other deeply, because love covers over a multitude of sins. ⁹Offer hospitality to one another without grumbling. ¹⁰Each one should use whatever gift he has received to serve others, faithfully administering God's grace in its various forms.

3. **What is the common theme found in these three passages?**
   The common theme is hospitality—inviting in and sharing with others, even strangers.

4. **What specific suggestions are given for practicing hospitality? List two ways these suggestions could be applied to visitors or newcomers at your church.**
   These passages suggest sharing food and drink; inviting in; sharing with those in need; serving others. Take time for some dialogue and brainstorming here. Encourage specific suggestions about how to apply these principles with visitors and newcomers.

Factors That Influence Welcoming and Enfolding

Review the following factors that can influence how a church welcomes and enfolds newcomers. As time permits, discuss which factors can be identified in your church and whether the influence is positive or negative. Encourage participants to jot down notes on pages 19-20 in their books, especially identifying things that apply to your church. Later in this session small groups will identify which of these factors play a role in your church.

Size

The size of a church can have a significant impact on a church's process of enfolding new members. Discuss the following patterns and ask which may be true of your congregation.

- *Small church* (up to 50 members)—enfolding a new member is somewhat like an adoption that key members or recognized leaders (often known as the "gatekeepers") must "sanction" in order for those people to really feel accepted. The enfolding ("breaking in") process may take longer, but in the end it usually results in a stronger family tie.
- *Pastoral church* (50-150 members)—pastor plays the lead role in leading a person toward membership and involving that member in the life of the church. The personality and charisma of the pastor is an important factor. Becoming a member is usually quite easy, but experiencing real fellowship may be more difficult because entry has been based upon a relationship with only one key person.
- *Program church* (150-350 members)—equipped members are key for coming into the church, which is usually through a formal program such as a Bible study, small group, or side-door ministry. If most of the programs are inward or maintenance focused, it can be difficult to find a way "in."
- *Corporation church* (350+ members)—usually some well-defined systems or processes are in place for getting into the church. You need to discover the right people and path to follow, but you can join without ever having developed any real relationships. It's easy to get lost or to purposely remain anonymous. It is easy for newcomers to go unnoticed and slip through the cracks because members allow the systems to assume their responsibility to reach out and enfold.

Carl George, in his book *Prepare Your Church for the Future*, compares churches of different sizes to the behavior of different animals. He estimates that 70 percent of North American churches fall into the small-church category, which he refers to as a "cat-size" church. These churches (like cats) are typically very independent, but operate with a clan mentality. His descriptions, which include characteristics of mice, lap dogs, yard dogs, horses, and elephants, give some interesting insights into the behavioral patterns of churches of various sizes.

History, Ethnicity, and Culture

The more ethnically distinct a church is, the more difficult it will be for "outsiders" to enter and assimilate. Many churches were started based upon the homogeneity principle—a shared history, ethnicity, and/or culture. People usually found themselves living in the community they did for the same reasons. That is no longer true. People move frequently and far and wide. While there is still a tendency to locate in a "like" neighborhood or environment, most churches that began as neighborhood churches find that their neighborhood has changed dramatically, perhaps several times. Ethnicity is described as a glue that bonds (something like "blood is thicker than water"), but even ethnic similarity doesn't necessarily mean a shared history and culture. Societal changes that used to occur over three or four generations now occur from one generation to the next. Churches that insist on maintaining their "uniqueness" as their bonding glue violate the principle of Galatians 3:28—"There is neither Jew nor Greek, slave nor free, male nor female, for you are all one in Christ Jesus."

Level of Christian Maturity

Our goal for Christian maturity is stated by the apostle Paul in Ephesians 4:

> *[11]It was he who gave some to be apostles, some to be prophets, some to be evangelists, and some to be pastors and teachers, [12]to prepare God's people for works of service, so that the body of Christ may be built up [13]until we all reach unity in the faith and in the knowledge of the Son of God and become mature, attaining to the whole measure of the fullness of Christ.*

It is obviously a good thing when we see more and more church members displaying Christian growth and maturity. It can, however, have a negative impact on newcomers if our growth, knowledge of the Bible, and experience in walking with God makes them feel inferior in any way. This can happen, for example, if your tradition has been strongly influenced by Christian day schools. It becomes easy to make certain assumptions or have higher expectations of new believers than we ought. We must remember that we all stand before God on level ground. We all are sinners, saved by grace.

At the same time, we must be prepared to minister to and design our programs for differing levels of spiritual maturity. While children raised in the church may be able to relate Bible stories from memory, some newcomers may never have heard them before. Obviously, we must not compromise our Christian beliefs or set maturity aside, but we must make sure it doesn't get in the way of developing healthy relationships that move others to maturity.

Age and Marital Status

People will naturally mix with those who are like themselves. This applies to gender, socio-economic status, ethnic-cultural identity, and even personality traits. It also applies to age and marital or family status. It is not unusual for people to be attracted to a certain church because it has many members who are in their age bracket and share similar family dynamics. Some churches abound with young families and small children, while others have a high percentage of elderly members or attract lots of single adults. This can be due in part to intentional programming or outreach. For the most part, though, it reflects the fact that people are more comfortable around others like them.

Not everyone has the option of going to a church where they feel a part of the crowd. Or they may choose not to do so because other things attract them to the church they attend. Because those who are different or in the minority tend to get left out, church members must make a concerted effort to give them extra attention. If it is not feasible to have special activities or programs that address their specific needs, then extra effort needs to be made to include them in the activities that do exist. It is surprising how far a little creativity can go in including everyone and it is rewarding to see how much everyone has to offer to the church.

Longevity of Current Members

Another area of blessing are the people who have been members of the church for a long time. Though this is not as big a factor as in years past due to our highly mobile society, it is probably more prevalent in rural churches and churches with mostly older members. The higher the percentage of members who have been together for a long time, the more difficult it will normally be for newcomers to become enfolded. In this setting a person can carry the "newcomer" label for quite awhile. All too often factions and tensions develop between the "old guard" and the "new folks" even though some of these new folks may have been attending for several years. A church that is experiencing this dynamic may want to see if any of its programs and activities tend to be exclusive. If that's the case, the church must make an effort to eliminate the natural causes for exclusivity and make including new people a high-priority goal. A church should be eager to discover which gifts, talents, and ministry God has sent its way through new people who regularly come to worship.

Other

See if you can identify other factors in your church that have an influence, either positively or negatively, on enfolding new members into your church family.

Small Group Activity

Break up into small groups. You may wish to use the same groups that you used in the last session. Have the groups spend about ten minutes identifying which of the factors discussed above can be found in your church. Hopefully, they've been noting some while the discussion was taking place. Have the groups address the following questions:

1. Do the factors we have identified have a positive or negative influence on enfolding? How?
2. What can be done to accentuate the positive influences or to eliminate the negative influences?

Have each group report back, noting key words on the overhead, whiteboard, or flip chart. After the findings have been listed identify recurring factors or suggestions (list each suggestion once and put a mark each time it is repeated).

Determine which seem to be the biggest issues and work one or two of the suggestions into achievable goals that can be addressed immediately.

Note: If you are pressed for time, you may need to assign one or two factors to each group; however, this may cut back on significant input others may have given.

Rating Our Welcoming and Enfolding Efforts

For this part you will need the summaries of the visitor, new member, and former member questionnaires. Share with the class an overview of the results from these questionnaires and have them compare their answers from the questionnaire they filled out for today's assignment (same as the second part of the new member questionnaire) and note any significant differences. It would be beneficial to have handouts of these results available and an overhead transparency that you can refer to as you discuss the questions below. You can do this with the large group or, if you have time, in small groups followed by reporting back.

Questionnaire Findings
Welcoming
1. What were the most common ways of finding out about our church?
2. What were the most common things that attracted people to our church?
3. In general, how did our members relate to these newcomers?
4. What were the primary descriptions of our church?
5. What is our church doing well in welcoming newcomers?
6. What areas need attention in order to better welcome people to our church?

Enfolding
1. What were the most common reasons for joining our church?
2. What two or three common suggestions were made regarding improving the way our church enfolds new people?
3. What elements were commonly present that made people start to feel accepted?
4. What were the most common reasons for people leaving our church?
5. What is our church doing well to enfold new members or frequent guests?
6. What areas need attention in order to better enfold people into our church family?

Action Plan
Based on the discussion about factors that affect your church and the questionnaire results, identify two specific things in the areas of both welcoming and enfolding that you can eliminate, change, improve, or initiate. Make one in each area a short-term goal (something that can be addressed immediately with little extra effort) and the other a long-term goal, which may require further planning and action before it can be accomplished.

Assignment

Encourage the participants to enlarge on the goals identified in the action plan with wording that would make them into definable, measurable goals. This should identify what is to be accomplished and a deadline. The "what" should be defined well enough so people will know when it has been accomplished. Some participants who are gifted in this area may want to identify more of the details by considering questions like the following, especially for the long-term goal: Who will be responsible? Are approvals needed? Are people, financial, or facility resources needed? Have them also reflect on how they might be personally involved in accomplishing these goals.

Closing Prayer

Be sure to request God's further guidance for your goals. Don't forget to praise God for the positive aspects of your church that have been identified.

SESSION 3

"Welcome to _____ Church. We're Truly Glad You're Here."

Purpose

This session focuses on welcoming guests. When people come to your church for the first time, do they receive a warm welcome? The Bible emphasizes the importance of welcoming strangers. In many places the Old Testament speaks of dealing rightly with the "alien" in our midst. Jesus goes so far as to say that our treatment of others—even those we don't know—reflects our treatment of him.

In this session we will talk about verbal and nonverbal ways to communicate a warm welcome and look at some practical suggestions for making meaningful contact with visitors.

Necessary Materials
- overhead projector with blank transparencies, whiteboard, or a flip chart
- markers

Opening Prayer

If you haven't already done so, by this point you should be able to invite someone else to open in prayer or encourage some sentence prayers focusing on the purpose of learning to welcome strangers.

Assignment

Take a few minutes to allow some of the participants to share their suggestions for specific goals that were developed out of session 2.

What God Says

Exodus 23:9
"Do not oppress an alien; you yourselves know how it feels to be aliens, because you were aliens in Egypt."

Leviticus 19:34
"The alien living with you must be treated as one of your native-born. Love him as yourself, for you were aliens in Egypt. I am the LORD your God."

Deuteronomy 10:19
And you are to love those who are aliens, for you yourselves were aliens in Egypt.

2 Chronicles 30:25
The entire assembly of Judah rejoiced, along with the priests and Levites and all who had assembled from Israel, including the aliens who had come from Israel and those who lived in Judah.

1. **What might make visitors feel like "aliens" when attending a new church for the first time? Is there anything about your church that may be unfamiliar or foreign to visitors from your own community?**
Ask if any of the participants have visited other churches. This would apply not only to those who have moved and looked for a new church; it could be experienced simply in visiting a different church while on vacation or traveling. Some of the factors identified last week can be mentioned here, such as ethnicity, age, and so on. Is the makeup of your church's immediate community foreign to the makeup of your congregation?

2. **The first three passages are from the first five books of the Old Testament and in the context of God's law to Israel. What other common denominator can you identify in these passages? Is the same true of you or your church?**

   The Israelites should have been able to empathize with being a stranger or alien because they lived that way for four hundred years in Egypt. Note that living somewhere a long time doesn't always make you part of the community. The Israelites were always aliens in Egypt. Find out how many people in the group can identify with feeling like a stranger. Does your church have a history of people joining so they could be with "their own"? Is having been a stranger something that helps or hinders your church's welcoming efforts?

3. **Look up the context of 2 Chronicles 30. What is the reason for the rejoicing? This was a very special, very Jewish celebration. What are some of your church's special celebrations? Are visitors (strangers) readily included in those celebrations? How?**

   This was a time of renewal for Judah under King Hezekiah. They were celebrating Passover and the feast of unleavened bread, something that only Jews could identify with. For foreigners to completely participate, they would have had to be welcomed. God wanted them to participate, not only in the celebration but also in the true meaning behind the celebration. Try to identify anything your church might do that would make visitors feel "really out of it."

Hebrews 13:2
Do not forget to entertain strangers, for by so doing some people have entertained angels without knowing it.

4. **Does the motivation behind this warning focus on angels or strangers? Explain your answer.**

   This is not intended to be a trick question. Our motivation should not be to inadvertently mistreat angels, resulting in some sort of punishment. The context of this verse is set in the need to love each other as brothers and sisters. Then we are also told to love strangers (in the same way we would respond to special messengers from God).

Matthew 25:31-40
31"When the Son of Man comes in his glory, and all the angels with him, he will sit on his throne in heavenly glory. 32All the nations will be gathered before him, and he will separate the people one from another as a shepherd separates the sheep from the goats. 33He will put the sheep on his right and the goats on his left.

34"Then the King will say to those on his right, 'Come, you who are blessed by my Father; take your inheritance, the kingdom prepared for you since the creation of the world. 35For I was hungry and you gave me something to eat, I was thirsty and you gave me something to drink, I was a stranger and you invited me in, 36I needed clothes and you clothed me, I was sick and you looked after me, I was in prison and you came to visit me.'

37"Then the righteous will answer him, 'Lord, when did we see you hungry and feed you, or thirsty and give you something to drink? 38When did we see you a stranger and invite you in, or needing clothes and clothe you? 39When did we see you sick or in prison and go to visit you?'

40"The King will reply, 'I tell you the truth, whatever you did for one of the least of these brothers of mine, you did for me.'"

5. **What was specifically done for strangers in this text? Who were the strangers?**

   That these may be strangers is mentioned specifically in the context of "inviting in." What are the implications of inviting someone in? In the context of the New Testament, it implied room and board and being treated with honor. It should be noted that all of the actions mentioned in these verses apply to our treatment of strangers. Strangers are people we don't know or to whom we have no affinity or natural connection. Reaching out to strangers requires stepping out of our natural circles and comfort zones.

6. **What does verse 40 suggest about our treatment of strangers? What is our reward for proper treatment of strangers?**

   The implication is clear that we are both representing Christ and responding to Christ in our treatment of strangers. Our reward is mentioned in verse 34. We are blessed of the Father and can come into our inheritance, which highlights the importance that Christ placed on the welcome of strangers.

Welcoming Principles

Discuss the following principles, encouraging participants to take notes in their books. You may find that some of the suggestions do not apply to your church's situation—for example, maybe your church doesn't use ushers. There may also be other welcoming strategies that you do use that are not mentioned here. Be sure to bring them up in your discussion.

1. Give Clear Directions
A visitor's questions

Try to put yourself in the position of a visitor or have participants think of visits they have made to other churches. List some of the first questions that come to mind (starting from when you enter the parking lot). Clarify these questions as much as possible. Be sure to address different perspectives (youth, parents of young children, elderly).

Where and how?

List ideas about when, where, and how information (answers to the questions just listed) should be disseminated. Do some brainstorming on this, and be creative. Don't let a "we've-never-done-that-before" mentality throw cold water on the discussion.

2. Initial Contact

Visitors may be . . .
- *wondering if they are welcome.*

  You may know that your church wants to grow and have new people become part of the church, but your visitors will not automatically know if they are really wanted unless that message is expressly conveyed to them.
- *anxious about themselves.*

  Don't assume anything. Everything may seem unfamiliar to your visitors and they may be unsure of what is considered "appropriate" at your church (this could include everything from attire to the correct way to respond throughout the service).
- *deciding whether to return.*

  First impressions are extremely important. The decision about whether to return to this church starts long before the service begins. Ask the participants to mention one thing about your church that would make them want to (or not want to) return if they were visiting for the first time.

Greeters should . . .

Whether or not you have official greeters, you should have people with the responsibility to make the following things happen. Simply assuming that someone is doing these things is a guarantee that they will not happen on a consistent basis. Which of the following does your church do well? Which has never been considered? Which may need some improvement?
- *be in place on time.*

  This means being in place before anyone else. Visitors, not being sure of themselves, may arrive quite early.
- *take the initiative.*

  Surveys indicate that 75 percent of us consider ourselves to be shy, inarticulate, and uncomfortable around strangers. Take the initiative to get conversations going.
- *be warm and friendly.*

  In the early days of Saddleback Church, a survey asked, Why do you think people don't attend church? One of the most common responses was that church members are not friendly to visitors.
- *be good listeners.*

  Listening is the best way to demonstrate genuine interest in someone else. Listening happens not only with the ears but also with the eyes and the whole body. Body language will tell a person if you are really listening.
- *give guests their time.*

  This goes beyond a simple greeting. It may mean spending less time with friends and others you know well. One solution to this is to introduce visitors to others you would normally chat with and include them in the conversations taking place.
- *look for special needs.*

  Be observant. Do the visitors need the nursery or directions to church school classes? Are there any obvious disability needs? Listen for special needs that may come up in a conversation. For instance, talking about work (often a conversation starter) may bring up an unemployment situation and some special needs.
- *acknowledge repeat visitors.*

  Try to remember names and pick up on previous conversations. If you don't remember a name, don't fake it; simply say, "I'm sorry, I know we were introduced last week, but I can't remember your name right now." Remind them of your name too. After a conversation with a visitor, make notes if you need to in order to remember. Yes, it is that important.
- *be ready to help late arrivals.*

  Someone should remain in the lobby or narthex of the church after the service begins to assist late arrivals. Chances are that they will already be somewhat embarrassed and flustered and will appreciate a gentle welcome and help, if needed.
- *continue their ministry after worship.*

  There is usually more time for visiting after the service. If you have a coffee time or other activity, be sure to invite visitors and show them the way. It's a good idea to station people by the exit doors as soon as the service ends because many visitors will tend to leave quickly. Try to catch them. If they are in a hurry, don't intrude on their time, but be sure to let them know you were glad they came and invite them back.

Ushers should . . .

Your church may not use ushers, but if it does, this is another opportunity to welcome guests and address any special needs. Ushers should give special attention to guests, making sure that they have a bulletin, songbook, handouts that may be needed, and so on. If possible, ushers should seat guests near people they might readily identify with and introduce them.

3. Plan Worship Accordingly

Different aspects of the worship service can positively or negatively influence how comfortable a visitor feels. You don't need to change things that are essential to your worship, such as the centrality of the spoken word, but there may be a number of nonessential elements that can be adjusted for the sake of the visitor. Some changes may force the current members to stretch their own comfort zones. This is where the congregation needs to make choices about how seriously it wants to attract and welcome new people.

Take some time to reflect on the things that your church can do or avoid doing in the worship service to help guests feel more comfortable. Some ideas are listed below, but encourage the group to come up with others that fit your context. You may wish to do this in two smaller groups. Have one group work on the "Do" list and the other work on the "Avoid" list.

Do	Avoid
recognize their presence	embarrassing them
announce the flow of the service	assuming that everyone knows what's next and what to do
announce page numbers	assuming Bible literacy
	using lots of unfamiliar, difficult music

4. Friendliness Is Everyone's Business at All Times

Sincere friendliness has its roots in love. Our passion for church growth must come from the same source as Christ's passion—a love for the lost. Friendliness without love is often a chore. Rooted in love, however, friendliness becomes a natural characteristic of any church.

Is your church a friendly church? Many would automatically say yes because they have friends there and other members are always friendly to them. Look around your church some Sunday morning. Are people smiling, shaking hands, and engaging in conversation? Now, check to see if visitors are receiving the same response. If so, is it from most of the people or are just a few folks naturally more outgoing? Friendliness has to be practiced. Nice people may not automatically be "friendly" and outreaching. Does your congregation need to be more proactive about welcoming guests? Take a few minutes to discuss the following:

Awareness
Members need to be on the lookout for guests, be aware of how they feel, and be willing to obey God's command to welcome them. How can you become more aware of visitors?

Initiative
Ask for suggestions for how initiative can be taken.

Follow-through
Specific follow-through could include making introductions to others, looking for repeat visitors, inviting them to sit with you and your family, and so on. Look for other ideas.

5. Guest Information

There are several ways to obtain guest information. Here are a few. What is your church currently doing? Is it effective? If not, how can it be improved?

Guest register
Rather formal, and works well only if it is strategically located (usually in the foyer), and guests are invited to sign without creating traffic tie-ups.

Information cards
These are usually located in pew or chair racks. Filling out the cards creates extra work for the visitor, and the cards can get lost if not completed in time to be put in the offering plate. Often the cards are filled out only by first-time visitors, making it more difficult to register repeat visits.

Friendship pad
Doesn't single out visitors and allows people in the row to catch names. It also allows a record of repeat visitors and opportunity to indicate other needs or interests.

Greet and welcome time
This works well if everyone is involved. Don't single out visitors by having them stand alone. Many visitors (64 percent according to one survey) will not stand or raise their hand in response to a general invitation to do so. It is important to make a second contact after the service with those visitors near you that you greeted during the service.

Four Basic Principles
1. You need *good information* in order to follow up well.
2. Do *not single out or embarrass* visitors.
3. Be aware of and *touch base with repeat visitors.*
4. Use a system that is *natural and appropriate* for your situation.

6. Church Information

Visitors need to have information about your church. This might include your church's vision statement, core values and beliefs, activities, ministries, and denominational or other organizational affiliation. Take some time to discuss what visitors need to know and want to know (remember, there is a difference—give them both) about your church and how best to disseminate that information. What is currently being done? How can it be improved?

What information is needed?

How should it be given?

7. Prompt Follow-Up

Prompt follow-up of visitors is important. You should find out ahead of time what the follow-up process is for your church. Then, looking at the possibilities below, determine which of these things, if any, your church does. What triggers that action (for example, a certain number of visits)? Is it effective? If you don't know, how can you determine its effectiveness? (You might have a partial answer to this question from the surveys you reviewed last session.)

Possibilities	Our Church
letter	
telephone call	
personal visit	

Principles
- promptness in touching base with visitors
- appropriateness (will vary with the visitor)—for instance, an out-of-town visitor would receive a different response than would an unchurched person living in the community
- a personal visit (does not have to be the pastor)
- each response should have a specific purpose—a letter, phone call, or visit should be short and to the point, stating your reason for the contact and your interest in them (as people, not numbers)

8. Other Fellowship Opportunities

Involving visitors in other types of fellowship opportunities is an excellent way to demonstrate your interest in including them in the life of the church. Take some time to list the possibilities that exist in your church. These could include things like small groups, Bible studies, coffee times, youth activities, recreational events, and so on.

Possibilities

When including visitors in other activities, you should be aware of the following cautions. Ask for some personal negative experiences that should be avoided.

Cautions
- Visitors are invited, but not included.
- Focusing just on the event and not the relationship (for instance, all attention is on winning the church softball game, and nobody reaches out to the visitor who was invited to join the team).
- Too much, too soon can be overwhelming—find the balance between sincere interest and pressure.
- Mismatching people because there is nothing appropriate for their age group or situation.

Initiating Contact and Conversations

Not all members of your congregation will be outgoing; for some, starting up a conversation with a complete stranger and keeping it going beyond the introduction stage is very intimidating. Here are a few suggestions. Encourage participants to share other ideas.

Openers

The most important openers are nonverbal: a smile, handshake, eye contact, and body language that doesn't suggest that you're about to do something else. The most obvious, easiest, and least threatening opening is, "Hi, my name is _____."

Comments

The most important element of any comment is its sincerity. Visitors will subconsciously be tuned in for the sound of sincerity. A simple comment is, "Welcome to [your church name]. It's good to have you here today."

Often in larger churches people are afraid of welcoming someone who has been visiting for some time. In this situation, a safe comment might be, "I don't remember meeting you. Are you visiting us today?"

Questions

There are any number of "safe" questions you can ask to get a conversation going. Some focus on interests: "Are you from this area?" "What type of work are you involved in?" "How did you hear about this church?"

You can also ask natural questions about possible needs: "Do you have any questions or is there anything I can help you with?" "Is there any way we as a church can serve you?"

Offers

Making offers to help can be an important part of a conversation with visitors: "Let me introduce you to _____." "Here, let me show you where it is." "Let me explain a little bit about what we have for kids your children's ages." "Just a minute, let me get an information packet for you."

Closing

"[Guest's name], it was good to meet you. My name again is _____." "Hope you enjoyed the service and that you'll come again."

FORUMS

The acronym FORUMS gives some ideas for conversations that begin to build deeper relationships with people. The word "forum" means a context for conversation. Note that there is a progression from more superficial topics to more spiritual. This cannot be canned or forced. Most likely, it will occur over a number of conversations as a more trusting relationship builds. Below are several ideas for conversation. Most people will find that once the conversation is off to a good start, it develops quite naturally.

Family

Are you married? Single? Do you have children? (Divorce and single parenting are common in our society. Be careful not to make someone feel inferior or unworthy, and avoid embarrassing or inappropriate questions.)

Occupation

Where do you work? Do you work outside the home? What do you do there? How long have you been doing that? How did you first get involved in that? I'm not sure what that is, what does it involve?

Recreation

Do you have any hobbies? We have a _____ group (team) here. Would you be interested in being part of that? How did you become interested in that? Did you have to have special training? What type of reading interests you?

U (You)

Be willing to share information about yourself, but don't focus too much on yourself. Listen for and talk about common interests, such as work, hobbies, children, and so on.

Meaningful

Ask for opinions and feelings about different things. Be willing to share your feelings.

Spiritual

Do you have a church home? Would you be interested in a Bible study group? Are you a Christian or is it something you are still thinking about? Are you interested in spiritual things? Do you have any favorite Christian authors?

Relationships are precious and sometimes fragile. We need to develop those relationships carefully, being sensitive about the questions we ask and being able to identify the types of questions that need to be asked.

Action Plan

Look back on the eight welcoming principles and see if there are any specific actions steps that you can implement. Have each participant list two things that he or she could do to be more welcoming. As a group list two or three things that the church could do to be more welcoming.

Assignment

Encourage each participant to put into practice the two things they have written down between now and the next session.

Closing Prayer

Thank God for your time together and ask God's blessings on your efforts to welcome visitors.

SESSION 4

Moving from Reaching to Enfolding New Members

Purpose

Making new and regular visitors feel welcome is a major accomplishment. A lot of work is necessary to attract new people. Programs to meet their needs, meaningful worship, appropriate facilities, and special invitations are links in the chain that attracts visitors. But all of our work is rather useless if people don't feel welcome once they come. Feeling welcome, however, is not the end goal. Ministry involvement and belonging is what keeps people in a church community. In *The Purpose Driven Church,* Rick Warren defines assimilation (enfolding) as "the task of moving people from an awareness of your church to attendance at your church to active membership in your church." This is a thought-out, strategic process. Warren goes on to say,

> The community talks about *"that* church," the crowd [visitors and regular attenders] talks about *"this* church," but the congregation talks about *"our* church." Members have a sense of ownership. They are contributors, not just consumers. . . . The incorporation of new members into your church fellowship does not happen automatically. If you don't have a system and a structure to assimilate and *keep* people you reach, they won't stay with your church. You'll have as many people going out the back door of your church as are coming in the front door.

The purpose of this final session is to study some of the dynamics found in most churches. We will identify the differences between presence, fellowship, and ownership—all different stages of full enfolding. We will also review some suggestions for enfolding, as well as enfolding patterns that the church is now using successfully. Finally, each participant will have an opportunity to put the principles of this course into practice.

Necessary Materials
- overhead projector with blank transparencies, whiteboard, or a flip chart
- markers
- copies of "My Part" questionnaire (p. 30) for each participant

Opening Prayer

Either lead in prayer yourself or ask one of the group members to do so. By now your group should be comfortable with each other. You may even ask for a few prayer requests related to lessons learned through these four sessions.

Assignment

Take some time to allow a few people to share their experiences with following through on the assignment from session 3.

What God Says

In several places the Bible speaks of the necessity of the people of God coming together in unity of giftedness and purpose. The apostle Paul uses the analogy of the body, emphasizing a oneness and unity in participation. The message is clear that every part is important; Christ's body cannot experience completeness or fulfill its purpose without unity.

1 Corinthians 12:12
The body is a unit, though it is made up of many parts; and though all its parts are many, they form one body. So it is with Christ.

Romans 12:4-5, 10
⁴Just as each of us has one body with many members, and these members do not all have the same function, ⁵so in Christ we who are many form one body, and each member belongs to all the others. . . . ¹⁰Be devoted to one another in brotherly love. Honor one another above yourselves.

Romans 15:7
Accept one another, then, just as Christ accepted you, in order to bring praise to God.

1. **What does the term "one body" mean to you? Do these passages focus on our uniformity or our differences?**

   One body implies working and functioning together in a way that allows the purpose of the church to be completed. It also implies a permanence—this is how God intended it to be. When one part suffers or a part is injured or missing, the whole body suffers.

   These passages speak to the importance of both differences and sameness—different parts, same body. Discuss the distinction between unity and uniformity. Unity is what these passages call for.

2. **What seems to be the key factor that allows for the oneness described in these passages?**

   Love. Christlikeness—note the terms "so it is with Christ," "so in Christ," "just as Christ."

Ephesians 4:4-13
⁴There is one body and one Spirit—just as you were called to one hope when you were called—⁵one Lord, one faith, one baptism; ⁶one God and Father of all, who is over all and through all and in all.

⁷But to each one of us grace has been given as Christ apportioned it. ⁸This is why it says: "When he ascended on high, he led captives in his train and gave gifts to men." ⁹(What does "he ascended" mean except that he also descended to the lower, earthly regions? ¹⁰He who descended is the very one who ascended higher than all the heavens, in order to fill the whole universe.) ¹¹It was he who gave some to be apostles, some to be prophets, some to be evangelists, and some to be pastors and teachers, ¹²to prepare God's people for works of service, so that the body of Christ may be built up ¹³until we all reach unity in the faith and in the knowledge of the Son of God and become mature, attaining to the whole measure of the fullness of Christ.

3. **According to this passage, how are we one, and how are we diverse?**

   We are one in body and Spirit. We share one Lord; profess one baptism; believe in one God and Father (vv. 4-6). We are diverse in that we share in a variety of gifts. Those mentioned here—apostles, prophets, evangelists, pastors, and teachers—tend to be communication and leadership gifts, but there are many more.

   Have each person mention one or two spiritual gifts that they have identified in themselves and list them all on the overhead or board. Afterward take note of how many different gifts there are just among this group.

4. **What is the ultimate goal of our oneness and the bringing together of such diverse gifts?**

   The ultimate goal (vv. 12-13) is to prepare us for works of service, which lead to unity in faith and knowledge of the Son of God. This, in turn, leads to maturity and attaining to the whole measure of the fullness of Christ. Discuss how enfolding people will help your church body fulfill that goal.

5. **What does the term "enfolding" mean to you? In what ways does it go beyond "welcoming"?**

   A thesaurus reveals several synonyms for the word enfold: envelop, enclose, enshroud, surround, enwrap, and invest are just a few. While we may think of enfolding as assimilation or blending in, we must resist that image. The church can and must experience true *unity*, but never by requiring *uniformity*. As individuals we retain our diversity in the one church. We are not called to a "cookie-cutter" Christianity. How boring (and unbiblical) the church would be if that were the case! Enfolding must take place as new people are introduced to opportunities for service in the church and are empowered to use their gifts for the building up of the body of Christ. This enfolding cannot occur without welcoming, but welcoming does not guarantee enfolding. The cost and effort necessary to welcome is minimal when compared to the ongoing effort and discipline required to enfold.

Levels of Inclusion

The student guide includes the same concentric circle diagram shown below. Briefly review each of the circles. If you would like to compare a very similar model and have a more complete description of each circle see the discussion of the "Five Circles of Commitment" in chapter 7 of *The Purpose Driven Church*.

Prospective Member Circle. Regular visiting nonmembers who have shown interest by their attendance or have a connecting link with the church through a relationship with a member or proximity to the church.

This circle is the largest because it includes both visiting nonmembers and potential attenders. This circle could readily

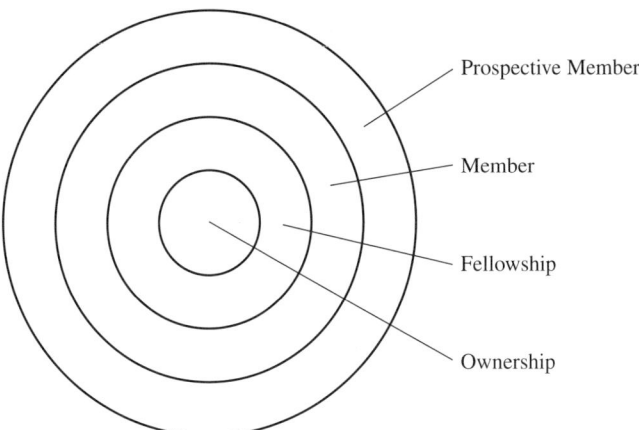

be subdivided to show those who are attending already and those who are part of your target group but do not attend.

Member Circle. Members who may regularly attend but have very little active involvement in the church's ministry and life.

These are people whose names appear on your church rolls, but who are not necessarily active or even regular in attendance. They are likely not involved in any small groups or the work of any of your church's committees or ministries.

Fellowship Circle. Members who are closely connected, have a definite sense of belonging, but are not deeply involved nor have any sense of "ownership."

These people have developed meaningful relationships with others in the church body. It has been said that a person needs to have at least seven others whom they consider to be friends before they will start to feel like a real part of the church. They attend worship services and other activities regularly and are likely to be involved in a small group, but they still tend to be more on the receiving end of ministry rather than doing ministry—for example, actively involved in Bible study groups but not leading.

Ownership Circle. Members who are highly committed to and involved in the life and ministry of the church.

These are the people who are most visible, have many friends, and are active in hands-on ministry. They often are in leadership positions involving both responsibility and decision-making.

If our ultimate goal, as expressed in Ephesians 4:12-13, is to prepare ourselves for [and do] works of service or ministry, then we will attempt to move all members toward the center circle of ministry. Obviously a growing church will always have people in the outside circle. As new people come in, each of the circles will grow as people develop in their personal commitment and involvement in the church. Churches must take care that these circles do not have walls. To do so, attention must be given to the special needs of those in each circle so they can keep moving toward the center. It would be good for your church to develop a means for periodically assessing what percentage of the greater body is found in each circle. The center circle should always grow in percentage as the church grows, but if any of the other circles begins to balloon, try to determine why people are getting stuck at that point. The church should also take note of what's happening with different groups of people, such as the young people, couples with young children, elderly people, or ethnic minorities.

Exercise and Discussion

Have participants put an "X" in the diagram on page 39 in the student guide to indicate where they feel they are now in the life of the church. Then have them put a dot to indicate where they were two years ago. Have the parents in your group write the initials of each child to indicate where they think their children are in relationship to their level of inclusion in the church.

Following are some discussion questions for further reflection, as time permits. It's a good idea to take notes of the discussion. You may want to draw the circles on an overhead transparency or the board to indicate where your group is and to identify any noticeable patterns.

Have you moved toward the center or away from the center in the last two years?

What factors have influenced which circle you are presently in?

What would help you move on to the next circle?

Are your children in the same circle as you? Why or why not?

What could help them move toward the center?

Are you and your spouse in the same circle? Why or why not?

How long were you in the various circles?

Which was the most difficult circle to "graduate" from?

You could also draw different sets of circles, each representing a different perspective. For instance, draw the circles according to percentages of people in each circle. You could also do a different set of circles for young people, elderly, young couples, minority groups, and so on. If you notice any pattern of people being stuck in one of the outside circles, you should ask why that might be. Perhaps you could also develop a simple survey of members from that group (for example, teens) to see if you are correct in your original perception.

Suggestions for Effective Enfolding

Briefly review the following ten suggestions for enfolding new members. Encourage participants to write down specific ways that they and/or the church could better address any of these areas. As time allows, give opportunity for sharing some of those ideas. For further study on the enfolding process see "Section Five: Building Up the Church" in *The Purpose Driven Church*.

Invite people to become members.

Don't make assumptions. People might not automatically realize that membership is expected or offered. Sometimes people simply need or want to be asked.

Intentionally reach out with the love of Christ.

One survey of four hundred people who had left a church indicated that 75 percent left because they felt that no one really cared if they were there or not. It is a demonstrable fact that if new members have not developed several friendships (six or more people) within the first six months, 70 percent will likely drop out.

Love is best expressed by genuine demonstration of caring. Don't wait for a crisis to come up before you reach out in care to new members. We all have needs all of the time.

Clarify the meaning of membership.

Make sure prospective members understand both the steps to becoming a member and what membership means. Are there different levels of membership? What about transfers or students? Is an interview, class, or public statement required? They should know in advance the church's position and their expected commitments in areas such as doctrinal beliefs, attendance, stewardship and giving, ministry involvement, small groups, and so on. They should also understand the privileges of membership.

Most churches have a membership class that discusses all these areas. Some churches have new members sign a covenant or agreement regarding membership expectations. The expectations should move new members in the direction of ministry and ownership.

Celebrate membership.

Make this an event. Let new members know that your church considers their joining to be important in the life of the church. Public acknowledgement, a simple gift in remembrance of the occasion, a reception line, and opportunity to give a word of testimony are all possibilities. If your church is a rapidly growing church with many new members, you can combine the receiving of new members on a regular basis and plan a bigger event.

One caution—some people will actually avoid taking the step of membership because they don't want to be singled out or embarrassed. Make sure that people know that exceptions can be made if they feel strongly about this.

Communicate your history, vision, and program.

Don't assume that your history, vision, and program are obvious just because most of the people have heard it all before. Make sure that new members are introduced to the history of the church, its memories, and the ways God has led.

New members also need to have the vision instilled in them. You will want them to share and own the vision for themselves. Don't assume that a neatly worded statement printed on the front of your bulletin has communicated to new members the heart and soul of your church's vision and purpose. Explain it. Tell how it germinated and grew. Demonstrate its biblical foundation. Develop enthusiasm to become a part of the wonderful vision.

Develop a means to communicate summary information on all the church's programs and ministries. This can be done well through ministry brochures or pamphlets. Be sure to include the names and telephone numbers of contact people for each of the programs. All of these things can be communicated in the context of a new members class. It is important that this class be well-planned, thorough, and required. There is no better time to convey the concept of expected commitment than a commitment to the new members class.

Purposefully stimulate spiritual growth in new members.

Expect new members to become disciples and to demonstrate spiritual growth. This will not happen by itself. The church must provide opportunities that meet different levels of need. It is not unusual for a new member to have little or no knowledge of the Bible, the church, or expectations concerning Christian behavior. Don't make assumptions or judgments.

Connect new members with a sponsor.

This is an excellent suggestion, although few churches have a formal sponsorship program for new members. A potential sponsor is someone who is spiritually mature, in the "ownership circle," knows and is deeply committed to the church, has a large circle of friends in the church, and demonstrates a Christlike love for people.

The involvement a sponsor will have with a new member will vary with the personality of each relationship, but here are some suggestions. Pray regularly with and for the new member; welcome him or her at your home; offer to accompany the person to church functions; introduce him or her to others in the church, and help the person discover a ministry opportunity that matches his or her gifts and interests.

Get new members involved in small groups.

If your church has a small group ministry, new members should be plugged into a group as soon as possible. There are many types of small groups. Some groups are focused on fellowship and are designed to provide closer pastoral care for each other. Others focus on study, ministry, music, prayer, support, or any number of other areas.

Small groups help to build meaningful relationships and allow sharing at deeper levels in a more intimate, less threatening environment. They offer opportunities for giving and receiving ministry that otherwise might not be readily available in some larger churches.

Small groups need maintenance in order to remain effective and directed toward the purpose and vision of the church. They also can become difficult to break into, causing small divisions in the church.

Provide a ministry.

New members need to find their place in ministry as soon as possible. If new members don't feel needed, they will either become inactive (go into hiding) or drop out. When people know they're needed, they know they belong. A proper match requires an assessment of interests, abilities, and giftedness.

Once a person is established in ministry, he or she needs to feel supported. This is accomplished through verbal support, appropriate training, a demonstration of interest, positive feedback, and prayer. Be careful not to overburden new members. This is easy to do when fresh people arrive on the scene, eager to find and establish their place.

Open up leadership.

Leadership must be reserved for Christians mature enough for the task, but that doesn't eliminate new members from leadership positions. There are different levels of leadership in the church. Leadership opportunities communicate to new members that they are trusted and important to the body. New members will bring new perspective and energy to your vision. They will also prove to be invaluable in understanding and ministering to other new or potential members.

"My Part" Questionnaire

Distribute a copy of the questionnaire (p. 30) to each participant. Ideally participants will fill it out and return it to you before this session ends; however, if they would like more time to think about a possible commitment, make sure you establish a deadline by which it must be returned.

The first option deals with serving on the Welcome and Enfold task force. Its work will be to follow up on some of the ideas that arose during these sessions. This group will be responsible for developing specific goals and an action plan for improving the welcoming and enfolding efforts of your church. This is an essential follow-up step. Without it, the time your group has spent together is likely to have no real impact. The task force should try to provide a recommended strategy to the appropriate leadership group within three months. Be sure to explain this option when you distribute the questionnaire.

Closing and Prayer

Be sure you thank the participants for their time and involvement in these four sessions. Encourage them to be intentional in welcoming visitors and enfolding new members into their lives and the broader church family.

Close with a prayer of blessing, asking God to make your church truly a loving home for every member of God's family.

My Part

Over the past four sessions, we have looked at the importance of effectively welcoming and enfolding people into the body of Christ. We have also looked at some of our own specific needs, strengths, and weaknesses in these areas. Obviously the task of welcoming and enfolding does not belong to just a few individuals in the church. It is the ministry of the whole church. Please carefully consider the possibilities below and indicate the areas in which you would be willing to consider helping. (*Note:* This is not a formal commitment at this time. We are simply trying to compile a list of possible resource people.) Make sure to include your name and telephone number at the bottom. Thank you.

I am willing to consider helping by

- ☐ serving on a task force that will develop and implement an action plan for improving our church's welcoming and enfolding efforts.
- ☐ serving as a greeter or usher.
- ☐ assisting at an information center.
- ☐ helping to design information brochures or pamphlets.
- ☐ following up with visitor contacts.
- ☐ helping with fellowship activities or new member receptions.
- ☐ helping with recreational activities.
- ☐ opening my home to visitors and new members.
- ☐ leading a small fellowship group.
- ☐ being a sponsor for new members.
- ☐ discipling others or leading a Bible study.
- ☐ leading a gift discovery class.
- ☐ other:_____

_____

Name _____   Phone _____

Continuing Task Force

The work of the Welcome and Enfold task force is not complete until something actually gets *done*. Your time and energy and that of the other participants is too valuable to be spent discussing needs, opportunities, and ideas and then doing nothing about them. The need for your church to become a truly welcoming and enfolding church requires appropriate action. Far too many good ideas for ministry never get off the ground because no one takes the initiative to develop a plan for implementing them.

This task force should do its work immediately, while the ideas and enthusiasm are still fresh. You should set a time limit—preferably no longer than three months—for accomplishing this work. Extending the time beyond three months limits the number of people who can commit to the task and risks the waning of excitement. Getting necessary approvals and implementing the recommendations may take longer, but that is beyond the assignment of the task force. Your immediate responsibility is to come up with an action plan that assesses the needs and presents a workable solution. It should be specific (so you know exactly what is to be done) and measurable (so you can determine if it is getting done), and it should be based on a vision of the ideal for your church.

Develop a Vision

A vision or stated goal regarding welcoming or enfolding may already exist, or it may be necessary to fulfill another part of your church's stated vision or purpose. If so, state the goal. Remind people that this is one of the driving forces for your church. If nothing exists, develop a statement that is God-honoring and provides a realistic goal for your church. Such a statement could read something like, "Every person who worships with us will feel welcome. Every frequent guest and member will be brought into a meaningful relationship with God and the church family." Obviously a vision or purpose statement is somewhat general; specifics for accomplishing the vision are contained in the action plan.

Review

Use the summaries of the preliminary surveys and any notes from the sessions to review your strengths and weaknesses. Make lists of everything good, even if it could be better. List everything positive, no matter how small or seemingly insignificant, that you want to keep or develop further. Do the same thing for weaknesses or things that need improvement. You may find several items appearing in both lists. Keep in mind that this is a brainstorming time. Put anything and everything that applies to your church on the lists. You won't be able (and shouldn't even try) to tackle everything. Later you can start to narrow down your goals.

Develop Objectives and Goals

Begin to group the items on your list. Start by separating out those items that pertain to welcoming and those that apply more to enfolding. You will have some overlapping here; that's okay. For instance, different groupings that you may have for "welcoming" might be
- things that deal with information.
- things that deal with personal contact with people.
- things that deal with comfort in the service.

Groupings under "enfolding" may include items such as
- opportunities for fellowship and making friends.
- appropriate activities for various needs and interests.
- discipling/spiritual growth.
- recognizing gifts and providing ministry opportunities.

These groupings will represent your major objectives. The different items in each group may become the various goals for working toward each objective. Some will be long-term goals, while others can be met in rather short order. An example follows:

Through the surveys and other class input, a weakness in the area of information to first-time visitors may have emerged. (It is a good idea to have a brief statement of purpose for each objective, indicating why this is being proposed.) An *objective* might read as follows:

Objective: To make information regarding the church and its ministries readily visible and/or accessible to any first-time visitor.

Purpose: To enable visitors to know the facilities and learn about the church without having to ask or discover by trial and error. This also offers a point of personal contact.

More specific *goals* under this objective might include
1. Post interior and exterior signs that identify or point to any area that a first-time visitor may need to locate.
2. Make sure all greeters are well-informed about activities (location, times, and so on) scheduled for that day.
3. Set up an information booth or table that is staffed before and after all services.
4. Update information packets describing the church and its ministries and make them readily available to first-time visitors.

Action Plans

Developing specific action plans is a matter of breaking down the goals into specific action that can be taken. Each goal may have multiple action steps, or it could have one very simple action. Since action steps need to be very specific, they should define several elements. Using goal 3, above, as an example, your action step would include

What?—To establish a central point that is readily visible and accessible to visitors where information is available regarding church activities and ministries and where specific questions that visitors may have can be answered.

When?—In place by the time the new fall programs and church school begin. (The time frame needs to be determined according to need. Having a time frame also makes the goal measurable.)

Who?—If possible, a person can be recommended to take responsibility for implementing this action step. This person may have to be appointed by the group in the church that approves the action plans. This person doesn't necessarily do the work, but he or she is responsible for assuring that it does get done by the deadline. This kind of ministry opportunity is an excellent way to pull someone into the "ownership" circle. It does not require someone who is already involved in leadership.

Resources—Resources involve finances, facility, and people. In this example, there may be very little monetary cost involved, depending on if you use some tables that are already available or build something that's more permanent. This action step may be somewhat dependent on the fourth goal mentioned above, the development of information packets. In that case, there may be some costs involved, but that would be requested as part of that particular action step. Facility would only be a matter of the actual space taken up by the information table or booth. Ongoing people resources would require a roster of volunteers at the information center before and after services.

You will notice that this action step relates with some of the others. If the information center needs maps of the building, that may fall under the action steps related to the first goal that deals with signs and other possible printed information regarding directions. The information packets fall under the fourth goal. The overall action plan should reflect the fact that action steps are often interrelated.

Someone with the gift of organization and administration will be able to lay out your action plan in a clear and organized manner. This can be done in an outline format or with charts and tables.

Measurement and Evaluation

A time frame is an obvious measurement indicator, but it may not help you evaluate how well the goal is being met. You may set up an information table in the middle of the lobby, but you might not be accomplishing your stated goal of disseminating information needed by newcomers. It is important that your action step be specific in terms of evaluation. It must define what you want to accomplish and how you will measure results.

It is also important to evaluate your new activities periodically. You should conduct a first evaluation within the first six months. One way to evaluate is to use the same tool or method that identified the need in the first place. For instance, if surveys of visitors indicated a need for better information services, then you may want to do another survey of visitors after your new information center is up and running.

Lest your task force become discouraged by the size of the task, remember you need to break it down into bite-size pieces (the action steps). You don't need to do everything at once! One important job of the task force will be to prioritize the needs. Whatever you are able to accomplish will be a step in the right direction.

Appendix A

Questionnaires and Survey Tools

This appendix contains some of the questionnaires and survey tools referred to in the "Groundwork" section. The Welcome and Enfold task force is responsible for gathering and summarizing the information that these questionnaires will provide. Copy these pages as needed to complete the pre-course analysis before the *Welcome and Enfold* study begins. Feel free to make adaptations and/or additions to the questionnaires and suggested surveys so that these tools best fit the specific needs of your church.

You should attempt to obtain as broad a representation of the people in your church as possible—men and women, different ages, ethnic background, marital status, and so on—to fill out the questionnaires. Don't look only for those who you think will give you "good marks." It is important to get an accurate view of the various perceptions about your church. If possible, each category of questionnaire should be filled out by at least ten respondents.

Make it easy for people to respond. It is best to provide a stamped, return-addressed envelope. If your church uses mailboxes, remember that visitors and former members will not have that option. If it is possible and convenient, the respondent may be asked to fill out the questionnaire while you wait. Make sure you let the respondents know the date by which you need the questionnaires returned, allowing yourself enough time to summarize the results before the first class session. It is also wise to keep a list of those who received questionnaires in case they have to be contacted and gently prompted to return them.

Visitor Questionnaire

The visitor questionnaire should be used with regular visitors, those who have visited your church a few times and would not be overwhelmed by your request to respond to the questions. This also allows them to give a fairer impression based on several visits instead of just a first impression.

New Member Questionnaire

The new member questionnaire is longer than the visitor questionnaire and will take longer to complete. Again, be sure to get a good cross section of new members to respond. If a new members class is in progress, that may be an ideal group of respondents. They also might fill out the questionnaire as part of their class time. Don't forget to get the impressions of young people too.

Former Member Questionnaire

It would be best if you can get permission from former members before sending them a questionnaire. If that is not possible, be sure to include a note of explanation and request for their help. In this case it would be appropriate for couples to fill out the questionnaires together. If you have not made advance contact, plan to send extra questionnaires because the percentage of return will likely be lower. Again, do not purposefully avoid former members who may have left the church because they were dissatisfied. You will especially want to hear their opinions.

Congregational Survey/Snapshot

There are several ways to collect statistics that give a picture of your congregation. These range from your own study of church yearbooks and the source information for those statistics, if it is still available, to hiring a professional consultant to help you do an in-depth study. One such consulting tool is the *ABC Church Resource Manual* (Christian Reformed Home Missions). The "Chapters in the Life of _____ Church" section will help you gather information key to understanding present and recent trends in your church. This collected data includes information on everything from growth trends to structure and work flow and giving patterns to financial indebtedness. This type of analysis is usually done in the context of a broader church study.

While this type of in-depth analysis is valuable in the overall planning process, it may not be necessary for the more limited purposes of this study. The "Congregational Snapshot" form is designed to guide you in identifying five-year membership trends that may be useful in discovering and correcting weaknesses or strengths in your current welcoming and enfolding efforts. It focuses on observing membership/attendance increases and decreases, the primary reasons for these changes, and how these changes have affected the "look" (age, ethnicity, income, proximity) of your congregation. You may want to identify other trends, such as gender or marital status, or eliminate a category if you know it doesn't apply to your church. It is very important that you are aware not only of the makeup of your church but also of significant recent changes.

Much of the information can be obtained through records available in your church office. The church's secretary or administrative assistant may help to provide some of the needed data. Gather whatever information your task force believes is necessary. The task force then needs to assess all the gathered information. If there are significant, observable trends, you may want to graph those so the class participants can see the changes and any possible connections.

Community Survey

The community survey will be valid only for churches that can identify a specific geographic neighborhood as a target area. Other churches will have to rely on sources such as Percept (U.S. only) for gathering demographic information. (To order this demographic information service, call Christian Reformed Home Missions at 1-800-266-2175, ext. 762. In Canada, you may obtain a demographic profile by calling Outreach Canada at 604-272-0732.) However, many churches exist in neighborhoods they no longer serve, among neighbors with whom they no longer identify. If a church truly desires to welcome and enfold its neighbors it will need to know who its neighbors are and what needs they have.

The community survey is another readily adaptable form that can be used as a simple assessment tool. It is usually best if surveys are done by teams of two. Be as unobtrusive as possible, and respect people's time. If your church has a simple brochure or other printed information about the church, make sure to bring it along and offer it to people who indicate that they have no regular church home.

The questions to be specifically asked are few, basic, and not overly personal. If you are able to strike up a conversation and learn some more, you can note the information later. Do not stop to write something down if it was not an answer to one of the survey questions. Use your eyes as well as your ears as you survey your community. You can learn much and answer many of the questions on the form just by "spying out the land" or prayerwalking through the neighborhood.

The task force should prepare a short (one-page) summary of what it would consider to be the church's immediate neighborhood or sphere of influence.

Visitor Questionnaire

Thank you for agreeing to help us assess how well we are doing in helping new people feel welcome to our church. We want to be able to see ourselves through your eyes. Please be totally honest in your observations about us, and use the additional space to add any extra comments. This will greatly help us to do the best we can to welcome others to our part of the family of God.

It would be most helpful if you would return this form by _____.

1. Why did you decide to visit our church? (check all that apply)
   ____ Mailing or advertisement (specify: _____)
   ____ Personal recommendation
   ____ Personal invitation by a member
   ____ Positive comments
   ____ Ministries that met my specific needs (specify: _____)
   ____ Curiosity
   ____ Other: _____

2. Did you have any difficulty finding the church or parking when you arrived?
   ____ yes ____ no (if yes, which: _____)

3. Were you greeted and made to feel welcome as you entered the church?
   ____ yes ____ no

4. Were there adequate signs (or people) to direct you once you were in the building (to nursery, worship center, classrooms, restrooms, and so on)?
   ____ yes ____ no

5. Did the ushers or others speak to you and give you any necessary assistance?
   ____ yes ____ no

6. How did other church members relate to you? (check all that apply)
   ____ smiled
   ____ exchanged names with me
   ____ hardly noticed me
   ____ gave a friendly greeting
   ____ engaged me in conversation
   ____ didn't seem to care that I was there
   ____ other: _____

7. Were you given an opportunity to register your presence?
   ____ yes ____ no

8. How did you feel about the service? (check all that apply)
   ____ I liked the sermon
   ____ prayer time was meaningful
   ____ I felt uncomfortable at times
   ____ I was inspired by the music
   ____ I was generally bored
   ____ I didn't always understand what was happening during the service
   ____ other: _____

(Please turn over)

9. Were you invited to return?
   ____ yes   ____ no

10. Why did you choose to come back again?

11. In a few words, please describe your initial impression of our church:

12. Please share any other comments that would help us understand your experiences as a new visitor:

Optional: Name   _____
          Age _____   Gender _____
          Occupation _____
          Address   _____
          Phone   _____

New Member Questionnaire

Thank you for agreeing to help us assess how well we are doing in welcoming and enfolding visitors and new members to our church body. We want to be able to see ourselves through your eyes. Please be totally honest in your observations and use the additional space to add any extra comments. This will greatly help us to do the best we can in welcoming others to our part of the family of God.

It would be most helpful if you would return this form by _____.

Your Experience

1. How did you first learn about this church?

2. What originally attracted you to this church?

3. What were your first impressions about the "welcoming attitude" of other members?

4. What were your first impressions of the church facilities?

5. How long did you attend before deciding to become a member? What were some of the key deciding factors?

6. Were there any "surprises" (positive or negative) when you became a member? (If so, please explain.)

7. When did you first feel accepted as part of the congregation?
   ____ first visit
   ____ during the membership class
   ____ when I became a member
   ____ still don't feel accepted
   ____ other: _____

8. What is the most satisfying personal experience you have had as a visitor or member of this church?

9. What is the greatest difficulty you have experienced as a visitor or member of this church?

10. What suggestions do you have to improve the way in which we welcome and enfold visitors and new members?

(Please turn over)

Rating Our Welcoming and Enfolding Efforts

Please respond to the questions below. Circle your answer, using the following scale:

5 = Very much
4 = Much
3 = Somewhat
2 = Very little
1 = Never
N/A = Don't know or not applicable

Welcoming

1. Our church has signs that make it easy for people to find their way around.   5 4 3 2 1 N/A

2. Our greeters and ushers help create a warm and friendly atmosphere before and after worship.   5 4 3 2 1 N/A

3. The various parts of our worship service (order of worship, bulletins, forms, language, and so on) are designed to help guests feel comfortable and included.   5 4 3 2 1 N/A

4. Church members are quick to greet, welcome, and talk with visitors.   5 4 3 2 1 N/A

5. We provide visitors a "non-pushy" way to register their presence, give information, and make needs known.   5 4 3 2 1 N/A

6. Everyone, regardless of social status, ethnicity, or any other characteristic, is equally and warmly received.   5 4 3 2 1 N/A

7. Members are quick to invite visitors or new members to their homes to visit or for a meal.   5 4 3 2 1 N/A

8. Visitors and potential new members can readily learn about our church's vision, beliefs, programs, and services.   5 4 3 2 1 N/A

9. A telephone, letter, or personal contact is made with first-time visitors within one week.   5 4 3 2 1 N/A

10. Opportunity for fellowship before and after the worship services is intentionally provided and encouraged.   5 4 3 2 1 N/A

Enfolding

11. Members of our church intentionally express love, acceptance, and care for visitors and new members.   5 4 3 2 1 N/A

12. Most of our members and frequent attenders feel accepted and have a sense of belonging in our church.   5 4 3 2 1 N/A

13. Specific opportunities are available for new members to get to know long-term members of the church.   5 4 3 2 1 N/A

14. Our church provides many good opportunities for new Christians and new members to grow spiritually.   5 4 3 2 1 N/A

15. Our church's educational ministries respond to differing levels of Bible knowledge, spiritual maturity, and religious backgrounds.   5 4 3 2 1 N/A

16. Visitors and new and long-term members have opportunities to participate in meaningful small groups.   5 4 3 2 1 N/A

17. New members of the church can readily find friendship circles or small groups that are open to them.   5 4 3 2 1 N/A

18. Members and regular attenders are helped and encouraged to discover and use their spiritual gifts in the life of the church.   5 4 3 2 1 N/A

19. The church's expectations regarding attendance, involvement, and finances are made clear to everyone, especially new or potential members.   5 4 3 2 1 N/A

20. All members—regardless of background—are expected to profess and demonstrate genuine faith in Jesus Christ and to actively participate in the church's goals and mission.   5 4 3 2 1 N/A

Former Member Questionnaire

Thank you for agreeing to help us evaluate our efforts to welcome and enfold visitors and members into the life of our church body. We want to be able to see ourselves through your eyes. Please be totally honest in your observations and any criticism you may have. Use the additional space to add any extra comments. This will greatly help us to do the best we can in welcoming others to our part of the family of God.

It would be most helpful if you would return this form by _____.

Your Experience as a Member

1. Why did you decide to join our church?

2. How long were you a member?

3. Why did you leave our church?

4. What was the most satisfying personal experience you had as a member of our church?

5. What was the most difficult experience you had as a member of our church?

6. What, if anything, could the church have done differently to make your experience as a member better?

7. In a short paragraph, please describe your impression of our church.

(Please turn over)

Evaluation of Enfolding Effectiveness

Please respond to the questions below. Circle your answer, using the following scale:

5 = Very much
4 = Much
3 = Somewhat
2 = Very little
1 = Never
N/A = Don't know or not applicable

1. The church intentionally expressed love, acceptance, and care for us (me). 5 4 3 2 1 N/A

2. We (I) felt a sense of belonging in the church. 5 4 3 2 1 N/A

3. Special opportunities were provided for us (me) to meet and get to know other members of the church. 5 4 3 2 1 N/A

4. The church provided many good opportunities for us (me) to grow spiritually. 5 4 3 2 1 N/A

5. The church's educational ministries responded to our (my) levels of Bible knowledge, spiritual maturity, and religious background. 5 4 3 2 1 N/A

6. We (I) had good opportunities to participate in meaningful small groups. 5 4 3 2 1 N/A

7. We (I) readily found friendship circles or small groups that were open to us (me). 5 4 3 2 1 N/A

8. We (I) were helped and encouraged to discover and use our (my) spiritual gifts in the life of the church. 5 4 3 2 1 N/A

9. The church's expectations regarding attendance, involvement, and finances were made clear to us (me). 5 4 3 2 1 N/A

10. As members we were expected to profess and demonstrate genuine faith in Jesus Christ and to actively participate in the church's goals and mission. 5 4 3 2 1 N/A

Congregational Snapshot

Membership/Attendance

Increases

	Current Year	Previous Four Years			

Source
- New believers
- Transfer
- Birth
- Other

Age
- 0-12
- 13-18
- 19-25
- 26-40
- 41-55
- 56-65
- 66+

Ethnicity
- African American
- Asian
- Caucasian
- Hispanic
- Native American
- Other

Economic (family unit)
- Unemployed
- Under $10,000
- $10-$25,000
- $25-$40,000
- $40-$60,000
- $60,000+

Proximity to church
- 0-1 mile
- 1-5 miles
- 5+ miles

Decreases

	Current Year	Previous Four Years			
Cause					
Transfer	_____	_____	_____	_____	_____
Death	_____	_____	_____	_____	_____
Lapsed/Removed	_____	_____	_____	_____	_____
Other	_____	_____	_____	_____	_____
Age					
0-12	_____	_____	_____	_____	_____
13-18	_____	_____	_____	_____	_____
19-25	_____	_____	_____	_____	_____
26-40	_____	_____	_____	_____	_____
41-55	_____	_____	_____	_____	_____
56-65	_____	_____	_____	_____	_____
66+	_____	_____	_____	_____	_____
Ethnicity					
African American	_____	_____	_____	_____	_____
Asian	_____	_____	_____	_____	_____
Caucasian	_____	_____	_____	_____	_____
Hispanic	_____	_____	_____	_____	_____
Native American	_____	_____	_____	_____	_____
Other	_____	_____	_____	_____	_____
Economic (family unit)					
Unemployed	_____	_____	_____	_____	_____
Under $10,000	_____	_____	_____	_____	_____
$10-$25,000	_____	_____	_____	_____	_____
$25-$40,000	_____	_____	_____	_____	_____
$40-$60,000	_____	_____	_____	_____	_____
$60,000+	_____	_____	_____	_____	_____
Proximity to church					
0-1 mile	_____	_____	_____	_____	_____
1-5 miles	_____	_____	_____	_____	_____
5+ miles	_____	_____	_____	_____	_____

Community Survey

Hi, we're from [name of church] Church, just over by [location]. We're trying to get to know our community a little bit better and find out some of the ways that we as a church might better be able to respond to neighborhood needs. Do you mind if we ask you a couple of questions?

Can you tell me how many people are in your family or living here? _____

How long have you lived in this neighborhood? _____

Are there any children living here? _____
    Gender _____ Age _____
          _____   _____
          _____   _____
          _____   _____

Do you currently have a church that you are actively involved in or any specific religious preference?

Do you have needs our church can help you with, or is there anything we as a church could pray about?

May I leave this information about the church with you?

Note: If they do not have a church home, be sure to invite them to the church. While direct questions may not be appropriate, through observation or casual conversation, you may be able to determine some of the following information:

Name _____
Race _____
Marital status _____
Estimated economic bracket _____
Employment _____
Names of children _____
                      _____
                      _____
                      _____
Address _____
Other observations:

Appendix B

Resources

These resources can be used to help you prepare to lead this course or for further study by your task force. Resources published by CRC Publications may be ordered by calling toll-free 1-800-333-8300 or through e-mail at sales@crcpublications.org.

Books and Articles

Admiraal, Henry. *Getting Together on God's One Another Plan.* Grand Rapids, Mich.: Church Development Resources, 1988.

Appleby, James, *et. al.* "Helping Guests Feel at Home." *Leadership,* Summer 1998, pp. 53ff.

Barna, George. "What Effective Churches Have Discovered: Insights on Ministry in the Late Nineties." Seminar workbook. Oxnard, Calif.: Barna Research Group, 1997.

George, Carl F. *Prepare Your Church for the Future.* Tarrytown, N. Y.: Fleming H. Revell Co.

Guidelines for Ushers and Greeters. Grand Rapids, Mich.: Church Development Resources.

Hart, Dirk. *Charting a Course for Your Church.* Grand Rapids, Mich.: Church Development Resources, 1987.

_____. *Hospitality and Assimilation.* Grand Rapids, Mich.: Church Development Resources, 1992.

Lauterbach, Mark. "Contact." *Leadership,* Summer 1998, pp. 34ff.

Loyd-Paige, Michelle. *Practicing Racial Reconciliation in Your Church.* Grand Rapids, Mich.: Church Development Resources, 1988.

McIntosh, Gary L. and Glen S. Martin. *Finding Them, Keeping Them: Effective Strategies for Evangelism and Assimilation in the Local Church.* Nashville: Broadman Press, 1992.

_____. *Finding Them, Keeping Them—The Seminar.* Forest, Va.: Church Growth Institute, 1994.

Schaller, Lyle E. *Assimilating New Members.* Nashville: Abingdon, 1978.

Small Groups That Work. Grand Rapids, Mich.: Church Development Resources, 1987.

Wagner, Peter C. *The Healthy Church.* Ventura, Calif.: Regal, 1996.

Warren, Rick. *The Purpose Driven Church.* Grand Rapids, Mich.: Zondervan, 1995.

White, James Emery. "Why Seekers Come to Church." *Leadership,* Summer 1998, pp. 49ff.

Data Gathering and Consulting Resources

ABC Consultations. For more information, call Christian Reformed Home Missions toll-free at 1-800-266-2175.

Percept data analysis (U.S. only). Call Christian Reformed Home Missions at 1-800-266-2175, ext. 762 for an order form. In Canada, you may obtain a demographic profile by calling Outreach Canada at 604-272-0732.